Bounce Back from Burnout

By Michala Leyland

Title of the Book by Michala Leyland

Visit www.woodforthetreescoaching.co.uk

Connect with Michala Leyland

Facebook www.facebook.com/woodforthetreescoaching

Twitter @wfttcoaching

Periscope @wfttcoaching

Disclaimer: To preserve the confidentiality of certain individuals described in this book, the author has not made reference to their names. This book is a reflection of the author's opinions. Whilst every effort has been made to support the reader through the burnout process, there are no guarantees of results. The author and publisher do not assume any liability to any party for loss, damage or disruption caused by errors or omissions. The author and publisher are not liable for the reader's subsequent actions, decisions or occurrences in their life.

This book does not replace the support of a qualified mental health professional. If needed this support can and should be sought by the reader.

"This book is 'Freakin' Amazing'. Michala's compassionate coaching style and great humour jump off the page despite being such a serious topic. A must read for anyone ready to transform their lives."

Lenka Lutonska, 'Get Fully Booked' Coach and CEO of Advantage Woman, creator of On Line Community Freaking Amazing www.advantagewoman.com/

"Heart felt and life affirming lessons presented in a down to earth way. Michala's warmth and passion comes through in every word. Every woman should read this book".

Nkechi Ajaeroh Amazon #1 Best-selling Author of Elevate Your Life, founder of @Afriscopetv
www.peristart.com

"Bounce back from Burnout comes straight from Michala's heart. Her dedication to supporting women avoiding being overwhelmed and living a full life is finally here in a book. Wonderful."

Cyndi Po, author of Life Actualised and CEO of Fit On The Go www.cyndipo.com/fotg

"I love Michala's common sense, solution focused approach to life, business and the definition of success. This book brings her voice to the page."

Jude Lennon, Disney Poet laurate, children's author, Judge for BBC Radio 2 500 Words and owner of Little Lamb Tales. www.littlelambpublishing.co.uk

"Michala is a true Woman of Worth. She delivers inspiring and solution focused messages to women across the world and this book is a true reflection of her dedication to celebrating woman and helping them see how wonderful and how worth it they are. A great read whether you have suffered from burnout or not. "

Janine Cummings #1 bestselling Amazon author of 'Everything', founder of international women's group Women of Worth #WoW and Award winning Motivational Speaker.

"Michala Leyland is exceptional when it comes to helping women avoid overwhelm. Her calm and open-minded approach makes her book perfect for anyone that feels stressed out. What makes her very unique is her positivity. There is not a problem Michala cannot help YOU solve. Michala will help you look for the solution until you find one. This book will start that journey."

Katya Varbanova Livestream Strategist, also known as LiveStreamKatya. Founder of Peri10k - An International Community of Change makers and Live streamers.
www.peri10k.com

Printed by Create Space. An Amazon.com Company

Content page

Foreword

Bibliography and On Line References

Foreword

Hello, freedom and clarity seekers. I am glad you can join me on a trip into the magical, mystery ride that is leading you to achieving the fullest of lives.

Now you find me in a good point in my life. I still only need my hair colouring every 6 to 12 weeks to keep the grey at bay! I have far fewer tantrums on my husband and children than I used to. (One day I'll be able to say next to none, but I'm not there yet.) I left a perfectly good, well paid job, and haven't regretted it for a second. I'm in good health and getting fitter by the day, with my new fitness goals rockin' and rollin'. Life's more centred, feels more in control and I'm more often in the zone (or nearly, no one's perfect.) as I have a mission and purpose in what I do with my days.

However, and it's a pretty big however, it hasn't always been like this. Several years ago I was a shadow of my former self. You may not have known it unless you were part of my family or a close friend. You'd have seen me and thought 'oh she's a confident chatterbox who seems happy in her own skin', and only occasionally would the cracks show. I'd look *really* tired (thank god for fake tan) or I'd not feel like engaging with anyone at the school gate, not like me at all.

Despite having a loving husband of 25 years (13 years married), two great kids, a loving family, a reasonably successful working life, a fabulous group of friends and no serious financial worries I felt overwhelmed, despondent and underappreciated. I felt like nothing I did was good enough for anyone, least of all me, and so I did what you need to when things aren't good enough I worked harder. Right?

I took on more activities, volunteered my time more, put myself out more for people. I convinced myself if I left my work it would fall apart (drama queen) and I stretched myself too thin. Or so I thought. I officially had 'martyr syndrome' and I didn't know it.

I began to feel resentful and point score at home. My poor husband! I was snappy and impatient with the children. I moaned a lot to friends (Thank you for sticking it out chaps! Sorry for being such an arse. LOL) how could this be when I had so much great stuff in my life? I must be an ungrateful person. Well no, actually, I had simply started on the road to '**Burnout'.**

'What is this burnout you talk of?' I hear you cry. Well, I imagine if you've picked up this book it's because you too feel like you might be in the middle of one or coming out the other side, am I right?

The Maslach Burnout Inventory[1] defines burnout as a three-dimensional syndrome made up of exhaustion, cynicism, and, eventually, inefficacy. Interestingly, during neither of my burnouts did I become ineffective, however, I perceived myself to be ineffective, which contributed to me working harder and longer to compensate for it. Has this ever happened to you?

Have you picked up this book because you are in the middle of a burnout, feel you may be in a burnout situation or you are over the other side of the raging fire stage and want to learn how to avoid it in the future? Whatever your reason I am so glad you found me.

Do or have you felt exhausted a lot of the time? Have you felt anxious in the place you work or doubted a lot of the decisions you've made? Have you isolated yourself from colleagues, family

---

[1] Maslach, C. (2016) Retrieved from https://www.researchgate.net/publication/277816643

and friends? Have you felt like you are the only person who is working hard and no one else understands how much effort you are putting in? Have you felt completely overwhelmed by the volume of work you have on your plate, that there aren't enough hours in the day, enough resources to achieve the task at hand? Have you felt completely demoralised by the lack of recognition, financial or socially, for the massive efforts you are putting into your job? Or, do you not accept the recognition that you are being given and fear that one day people will see the 'real' you because you doubt your abilities so much, despite others appreciation of your work?

If you have experienced some or all of these, it is likely you have experienced burnout. Obviously, there are varying degrees of burnout and how it affects you, but the three-dimensional syndrome is well recognised. What I love about this approach is that Maslach demonstrates how, by and large, burnout occurs because of a mismatch in the job that you chose and the environment you work in, not only simply as a consequence of a perceived individual weakness. That means my lovelies, there is hope!

"Burnout is not a problem of individuals but of the social environment in which they work. ...A good understanding of burnout, its dynamics, and what to do to overcome it is therefore an essential part of staying true to the pursuit of a noble cause, and keeping the flame of compassion and dedication burning brightly."

[2] I couldn't agree more. In hindsight, my burnout in teaching was rooted in the volume of work teaching French and English, two subjects which have major demands in regard to marking and lesson preparation. In the charity sector, my burnout was rooted in lack of resources and limited delegation opportunities. Although, I also firmly believe that on an individual level there is a

---

[2] Maslach, C. & Leiter, M.P. Reversing Burnout. How to rekindle your passion for your work. P44 Retrieved from http://www.newchaptercoach.com/wp-content/uploads/2008/11/activist-burnout-article1.pdf

lot we can do to strengthen our mind muscles in order that we can stay in those environments if we wish to, as you'll soon find out through the activities you are about to undertake.

This book aims to first clarify what is causing *your* burnout symptoms and where *your* mind set isn't supporting *you*.

Second, it will help you pin point how *you* can appreciate *you* more, grow to love *you* for *you*, warts and all.

Finally, it will help you find an environment that meets *your* needs by achieving *your* vision, mission and success definition, having created a way of thinking that will help *you* thrive, not strive all the time. It will help you assess if there is change that can be made within the environment you are currently in or if it's time to move forward and create an exit plan that allows you to thrive. Sound good?

It's only in hindsight that I can see burnout is a great opportunity.

(And we all know hindsight is a great thing!) Chances to reflect, review, assess; what are you doing and why?

As I have mentioned, my first burnout happened to me in the late '90s when I had been a young teacher for several years, and because I have a high achiever saboteur, but I'm not stupid, I knew that the belief I've always held from a very young age, needed to come into play before I dragged myself, and my family, to a level of misery unknown to man. (I'm prone to exaggeration, it can work for me and against me. Strength in weakness shall we say?) Or at least I'd burn myself out and become mentally or physically ill. Not going down that road!!

I didn't take that path. I listened to my mind and body and I acted on the feelings. The belief, "If you always do what you've always done, you'll always get what you've always got", kicked into play.

I decided I needed to find a different way. I needed to start looking at the choices I have. I needed to begin to appreciate today and what I have, rather than stressing myself out worrying about past mistakes, or worrying about what might happen in the future.

Let's face it we all make mistakes, that's how we learn and we can't predict the future, no matter how gifted we might be.

Six or seven years ago I'd attended a weekend workshop for aspiring Life Coaches. I knew then in that room that that was my purpose in life, but I'd just had two babies in quick succession in my mid 30s and the timing wasn't right for me, or at least I thought. (There is a lesson in that I feel, but we'll cover that later.)

It started me on a path of reading more about personal development. I found Tony Robbins, god love him, Fiona Harrold, reintroduced myself to Dale Carnegie etc. I am a big believer in lifelong learning. I love signing up for courses that give me more knowledge and understanding of people and how we tick.

Later, I started a Life Coaching accreditation to expand my coaching skills from the classroom and training rooms, but work ramped up, being the primary local carer for my ailing nana, her subsequent passing, whilst juggling two toddlers, took me away from what I knew to be my true purpose in life. I just couldn't see the wood at all. Finally work was draining me of all my positive energy. There were some people I loved working with, but the achievement of working in a senior management role took me further and further away from the very thing that makes my heart sing. Job mismatch? I think so!

Helping people to make positive changes, supporting people to achieve their potential and knowing that my caring, giving, positive energy was having a direct impact on people's lives, face to face, wasn't being used. It's why I had become a teacher (Naïve? Perhaps in the current political climate). It is why I worked in the charity sector for over 12 years delivering coaching and training in business and education. I was born to help people be the best they can be and I'm good at it.

I've even coached a cashier in a supermarket queue to consider taking a beautician course at the local college. Her stunning eye makeup caught my eye. She had a gift, I felt compelled to talk to her about it and amazingly she had never considered it as a career option and couldn't see how talented she was. Next time I saw her she'd signed up for night school and was watching YouTube tutorials in the meantime. I can't help myself. LOL.

We all have a gift and I know mine is to see the beauty within someone and help them to see it too. I can help them to achieve their potential and become the best version of them that they want to be. I knew I had to get out of the management rat race. I knew it wasn't nourishing my soul. In fact it was depleting it. My family were on the edge. My emotional energy for my kids had become limited, one of my children was suffering, and my emotional energy for my husband was at negative 20. (I still wonder to this day how he managed to stay around. Sorry. I love you) I'd started to doubt myself again, having felt confident and competent for many years.

I left my job with an idea, a vision and a vague plan, but most importantly with the support of the love of my life. At first, I needed to find out exactly what I needed to do to set myself on the path that would lead me to you. For over two years now I have been on a wonderful journey discovering all the possibilities to produce a clearer, calmer, more appreciative life. Don't get me wrong it's not all rainbows and singing from the tops of mountains

(I do love a bit of that!) but it is a million miles from the deep dark woods I used to be flailing around in.

I started Wood for The Trees Life Coaching in January 2015 and I haven't looked back. (Well, only to review the first year with a constructively critical eye) It's exciting, it's energising, it's freeing and by jingo, I want to share that feeling with you.

Consequently, my obsession with tree and plant metaphors will be peppered throughout this journey through the woods we are about to take, but I am certain you are going to love them.

So, get your slippers off, you won't need those. Get your wellies on and let's tramp through this big old forest and see if we can get to the other side of the woods together. ('And if we don't?' I hear those entrenched among you cry. Then we tried and we will look for another way, a different way until we flippin' well do. What's the alternative Mrs?)

I know how you feel. I know how hard it is and I'm right here next to you, holding your hand, or kicking you up the backside, and walking through the woods to a freer, clearer, more content you. If I can do it, there is no reason you can't.

Spoiler alert and disclaimer: This isn't a book that is going to work on you by osmosis. The activities have to be **completed** for you to get the most out of it. If you are going to just read the questions ask yourself this:

Why aren't you worth the effort of thinking things through and putting pen to paper?

What needs to happen to make you worth taking a few hours of your life to think about how you can be the best version of you and make the most of what you have to gain the fullest life or to appreciate more the full life you already have?

I'm not a psychologist, a counsellor or a medical professional. I am a woman who has experienced burnout who is on a mission to remove the taboo from speaking out about the fact that it can happen to anyone. I want to use the tools and techniques I have learnt as an accredited coach help you take steps forward and use this time to plan a future that is brighter.

So, what are you waiting for? What have you got to lose? Are you with me? Yippppeeee. We're off....

Section One – Disco Inferno!

Ok, so here's the tough part. We're going to look at where you are right now. As I said I am NOT a counsellor. If you need to unpick the past and understand how that has impacted on you, I strongly recommend you seek professional help and take the brave step to understand those patterns of behaviour at the deepest level. This is about NOW. What, who, why is something stopping you NOW from living the life you want to live or enjoying the life you have? It's a different set of questions, with a different set of answers, and ones you may well need to answer, but this is about the present.

Let's get this party started.

In this first section we will look at things as they are. You've been in burnout, you're out the other side feeling wounded? Wherever you are we're going to look at what the key issues you have right this minute. What is bugging you now? What are the main issues facing you today? How are you talking to yourself about these issues? What habits and routines are keeping you stuck? Who is impacting on your life and in what way? How is your current thinking helping or hindering you?

This part of the book is going to get you deeper into the darkness of the woods before we start to forge towards the clearing. There may be times you don't want to face the truth, or the negative voice will rear her ugly head, but don't let your avoider saboteur take charge. It's OK to look at these issues, because together we will find solutions. If you are willing to do the work, of course. I'm not talking about studying the worms or rooting about in the roots, like I said that's the job of a counsellor. What we can do here is pull out weeds, chop off dead wood and prepare the soil for regrowth. We use the past as compost. It will feed our development today, but we won't get up to our eyes in it.

It's useful to learn from our mistakes but we won't dwell on them as it's counterproductive at this point. We'll do all this with my Merseyside humour dotted throughout and a million tree metaphors. I've also highlighted many of the personal development readings, videos and resources that have helped me on my journey, for which I am eternally grateful. I hope you enjoy them too.

Before we start we need some quick preparation. Make sure you are comfortable; temperature and clothing. You'll need a little book or some paper to write in or if you prefer you can type up your answers. Personally, I like a lovely notebook to collect my thoughts, but I have got a stationery addiction issue. LOL

It's always good to clear the mind with what I call 'Clearing breaths'. (See what I did there?) They bring clarity. An essential part of avoiding overwhelm is breathing, and to take that a step further, a daily practice of meditation which allows you to connect with the breath, and focus on simply being, is essential to long term emotional resilience. Major studies have been completed on this and there are some fantastic apps to download such as

'Headspace' or 'Calm,' and Deepak Chopra's 21 Day Challenge is a great way to start if you want to really work your mental muscle. In his book 'Positive Intelligence'[3] Shirzad Chamine discusses how to increase your emotional intelligence through this mindful practice. He examines how by being mindful in moments our sabotaging thoughts kick off; we can build the 'Sage' side of the brain which allows us to be more creative, empathetic, and resourceful. There are lots of great meditation and mindful YouTube Videos for free too, but quite simply, it just needs you and your breathing to clear your mind.

---

[3] Chamaine, S. (2015) Positive Intelligence. Greenleaf Book Group Press. Austin TX p103

Clearing your mind of all the day to day chatter. Clearing your mind of the Mean Little Cow Voice. Clearing your mind of all that was and all that will be, to simply here and now.

Chapter One –Out of the Woods

Right then, let's start this journey together. Be really honest with yourself and identify what is making you feel exhausted, resentful, overwhelmed, and foggy. However you are feeling, you need to identify *exactly* what it is before you can take action to sort it out. Knowing if it is your environment, the people in your environment, the level of work satisfaction you have, your own mind set and perspective will support you avoiding burnout moving forward. It will help you know if it is a change of work place, job role, additional support, self-care, resources or perspective that is needed moving forward.

I start all my client sessions with this important Clearing technique, as explained in the Section One introduction.

Have your eyes closed and gain good upright posture. Do at least 5 and really clear the lungs, more if you need to. Deep breath in through the nose, deep breath out through the mouth until you feel comfortable that you are present with this activity. Do this Clearing breath at the beginning of each exercise to get clear and gain the head space you need. Now we will begin.

Give yourself at least an hour for this or break it down and look at individual issues in 30 minute blocks.

What issues/situations/people are bothering you at the moment? Why?

How does this affect you?

What would you like the issue/situation to feel like if there were no challenges/weeds in the way?

What have you done so far to resolve the issue/situation? (If nothing, say nothing. The only person you are kidding is YOU.)

What challenges do you face in dealing with the situation/issue?

Which ones are in your control?

Which ones are out of your control?

Are there any actions you can think to take right now to improve the issue/situation?

Anything else? (Be creative)

When will you do them?

Get out your diary/calendar and set a date/time for the action. If you are resisting starting, question why?

What are you scared of?

How can you work with that fear?

What one step can you take now despite that fear?

Take your time over this exercise. You've found out what's happening, who's involved, what problems/barriers you are facing and you've started to look at solutions.

If there is more than one issue/situation **repeat the exercise**. If you get stuck, stop and repeat the Clearing breaths. If you are struggling to get creative, leave it and come back to it remembering to do the Clearing breaths before you start to look at it again. However, if you have taken the time and trouble to write down some answers, trigger a time to come back to it and act on it, as it must be important to you. Am I right?

The next stage is going to be getting you into a good state of mind in order to bring 'best you' to the party more often, no matter what environment you are in.

Chapter Two- Suspicious Minds.

Ok. So if you've read my blog you'll have heard me mention my "Mean Little Cow" (MLC). She's the sneaky little voice that tries to sabotage my efforts when I am getting out of my comfort zone or if I am feeling like there aren't enough hours in the day. Or god forbid I should 'get above my station.' She's my fear! Fear of change. Fear of risk. Fear of living the fullest life and the situations that might put me in. (She was right to fear the day I took over an abseiling challenge for a friend who's phobia kicked in. Maybe should have listened to her then! LOL)

Everyone has a MLC it's the subconscious side of the brain that functions on our fear and self-doubt. It depends how well trained it is, as to how loud it is in your head. When we are in a burnout situation it can be at its most vocal. Sadly, this is a time when we need it to be at our most logical and conscious! We can lose all sense of perspective and the ability to be solution focused, because MLC has us listening to our fear and doubt *too* much.

Having said that in this section, I want you to listen to your "MLC" over the next few days. And identify when she gives you back chat and what exactly is she spouting? When you get really good at this you will hear that there are several different voices to MLC or 'saboteurs' and as discussed, I highly recommend the work of Shirzad Chamine[4] to understand this on a deeper level.

For some people she's not very loud. For others, she is screaming in your ear. Whichever way, find out what she is telling you and then in Chapter 7 we'll undo her evil deeds. First things first, breathe. Clear your mind of anything keeping you foggy. Concentrate on your breath. Now to work, complete the table overleaf with your findings.

---

[4] Chamaine, S. (2015) Positive Intelligence. P16

"You are YOU. That is your strength."

Michala Leyland

Remember she is a cow, don't believe her!

When? Most common time she pops up.	What does she say?
Example: When I'm overtired	You are a rubbish mum, all you do is shout.

Right. How's that "mean little cow" working for you? Is she inspiring, energy giving, joyful, pleasurable, encouraging? Or is she just a mean little cow? For me, at her worst, she does the opposite of everything I have just mentioned. She's demoralising, exhausting, miserable, painful and discouraging. So what the *hell* are we doing listening to her and believing her?! **Really?**

We are intelligent, vibrant, passionate women. We wouldn't allow someone else to speak to us in this way so why do we do it to ourselves? The emotional or 'Chimp' part of the brain, as explained by Dr Steve Peters in The Chimp Paradox[5], is there to help protect us in a survival situation. Unfortunately, if we focus too long on this part of our brain it will send us messages that make us doubt ourselves, our abilities, the circumstances we are in, that is your Mean Little Cow voice.

---

[5] Peters, S. (2012) The Chimp Paradox: The Mind management Programme. Croydon. Vermillion. P30

In burnout she is in overdrive!

It's important to hear the signals our 'Mean Little Cow' is giving us, but it is more important to act on what she is trying to tell us, rather than linger on it.

In Chapter 7 we'll look at ways to undo this damage. She's keeping you stuck, she's stopping you from enjoying what you have now in your life, she's making you fear success and she is terrified of failure. She's stopping you from achieving success in a way that lights you up and keeps you foggy and misty on how you can bring more of it into your life. She's keeping you in burnout. By listening to that MLC voice for too long you are not taking advantage of the other side of your brain that is empathetic, imaginative, creative, resourceful and investigative. She's trapping you in her negativity and it is time to train her to be quiet. You'd think I'd be saying let's kill her off, but sadly she does serve a purpose. As humans we need to be able to identify danger and risky situations but when we let that voice dominate we simply reduce our experiences to risk adverse, doom laden nonsense, and we don't want that do we?

Therefore, keeping a regular ear on what your MLC is telling you and then acting on the grain of truth, and ignoring the rest, will keep her quiet, but doing the job as is meant to do, keeping you safe from real danger not making you feel bad about you a lot of the time. Now, I realised in both my jobs that MLC had been trying to protect me from the fact I was in roles that were a mismatch to my personality and needs but unfortunately, I didn't listen to her in an action signal way at the time. I simply listened to her and she made me doubt my abilities and my competency. I'm so glad you have found this book because you can learn to listen to her with a conscious ear.

Chapter Three – OOPS I did it again.

Next we need to look at our unproductive habits. Sorry. I know this is hard, but if we identify them we can do something about them. If looking at your negative habits seems to contradict what

I've just said about believing your "Mean Little Cow", let me explain why it isn't.

The negative habit might be listening and believing the negative voice.

It might be eating foods that don't nourish you or give you lasting energy.

It might be shouting at your children or partner instead of talking in a way that would encourage listening, love or independence.

It might be leaving tasks to the last minute and feeling anxious and overwhelmed as a consequence.

Whatever it is, or whatever they are, will not help you feel good about you or to grow and develop into that strong, lush oak you deserve to be. In fact those habits are food for thought for that

MLC. Eating badly? "You are a fat, greedy pig." Shouting at the kids left, right and centre? "You are a horrible mum, you don't deserve kids." Going to bed late at night? "You are pathetic, you know you need more sleep, you've no discipline." Do you see what she does she latches onto the bits of evidence but then attacks you for it? Sometimes, there might be a grain of truth in what she says and you can use it as a signal to act on, but listen to her too long and she will drag you down and keep you stuck.

> *"Listening to your 'mean little cow' voice for too long will result in you staying stuck. So don't!"*
>
> *Michala Leyland*

So again, grab a cuppa. Take a breath and be honest. This is for you and only you. Look at what negative, unproductive habits you have. Eventually, you can find a way to make changes that will cause you to blossom. Write them around the cloud to keep them contained in this space.

Take as long as you need.

However, before you start do some Clearing breaths.

Well, I think you should stop picking your nose now as that benefits no one! HAHA!

But, seriously we'll look again in Chapter 8 at these unproductive habits and identify ways you can introduce positive, productive habits/routines that get your juices flowing. It's so important to look at what is helping or hindering you as by making small shifts, in thought or deed, you can dramatically change the course of events. Even when there are mismatches in the environmental situation you have in work or life shifting your perception can alter your experiences.

For example, I had a client who we established had a self-limiting belief that the only way to comfort herself, when she was feeling sad, burnout or angry, was by eating huge amounts of chocolate. Furthermore, she ate when she wanted to reward herself too! It was what happened as a child when she was upset she'd be given food to comfort her or as a reward. She came to me upset that she couldn't maintain a healthy way of living despite various attempts at diets and exercise plans. By identifying this behaviour she made a subtle change by creating a new belief. This new belief was so simple but so powerful. She started to believe that when she wanted to comfort or reward herself she could chose to do it by choosing a different reward. She could choose to pamper herself with a nice essential oil bath or a manicure. She could comfort herself by speaking to a friend or going for a long walk. In doing so she felt that she was taking pride in her appearance and looking after herself inside and out. Consequently, it helped her eat more healthily too which resulted in increased energy levels and weight loss.

It was only a tiny shift in thought, but by being conscious of the behaviour, and the belief behind it, she was able to rewrite the belief and change the behaviour.

There may be habits that you are engaging in that emphasise the challenges you face in your working environment. For example, you may feel the need to help everyone in the team and always say yes when someone asks for help or wants to delegate a task. Do you ever consider what the impact of saying yes will have on you?

Perhaps you have a boss who communicates differently to you and you have a habit of communicating in your style which doesn't help you gain the support and additional resources you need. Is is possible to adapt your communication style to gain for out of these interactions.

I am not saying all of what is happening is down to you, the boss may well need to consider adapting her/his communication style too, however, I am saying only you can change the habits YOU are responsible for and you owe it to you to do it.

Now, we've got closer to what is making you burnout, feeling fed up and keeping you foggy let's leave those negatives here. It's time we'll crack on exploring what's going on in the woods before we start finding our way into The Clearing.

Chapter Four – Things can only get…

Another big problem for 'busy' women is the feeling of being overwhelmed. That feeling in the pit of your tummy, that there aren't enough hours in the day. Being 'busy' has become a badge of honour for many of us. I know I wore it for a long time. In fact, there is a belief that has been generated in western society, that if you aren't busy *all* of the time then you aren't doing it right.

"It's not enough to be busy; so are the Ants. The question is: What are we busy about?"

Henry David Thoreau

WRONG!

Being too busy with things that aren't important to you, or are filled with *all* the things you 'should' do because someone, (your mum; your partner; your family; your community.) has made you feel like you should do it, will only fill your days with dread. It will leave you with too much to do with no direction, no clear boundaries and a feeling that whatever you do is not enough. It can lead to burnout. Is that what's happened to you?

Everyone has the same 24 hours in a day so why do some people make it look so effortless?

Here's a little secret; a lot of women make it 'look' easy but are swimming like swans underneath. The rest of them make it 'look' easy, but they aren't actually *doing* half of it! The nanny is sorting the kids; the cleaner/housekeeper is on top of the house. They may have a PA who sorts out everything at work. Now, this level of support only comes at a certain level of income and I personally applaud these ladies for seeking out and accepting that help. For most people we're juggling a lot of 'stuff' and it's not a stretch to realise your arms will eventually get tired *and*, eventually, a ball or two will drop.

The aim is to stop being busy. Busy is easy to achieve. Busy can happen with little effort on your part, but a full life and a fulfilling life are harder to achieve. Therefore, we need to look at what takes up the majority of your time and what is draining the nutrients from your beautiful roots. First things first, breathe. Clear your mind of anything overwhelming you in there.

Concentrate on your breathing for 5 deep Clearing breaths or more if you need it.

Use the circle below as a pie chart to show what percentage of time various activities fill your average day right now.

Or, if you prefer, use this table to record the activities in hours per day or week.

Activity	Hours in the day or week

Categorise the areas. Housework, Work hours, Social Life, Social Media, Entertainment, they will depend on you and how you spend your time. Once you've done this you can start looking at the reality of what needs to change, if anything.

What can you stop doing?

What are your time vampires? (Be honest!)

What can you start looking to stop doing if you plan it well and gain the right resources to make it happen?

Who can you ask to help/support you or delegate to?

What can you start doing?

If we are really honest with ourselves, a lot of us find it hard to give up control, set perfectionist, sometimes dare I say, unachievable standards, set no boundaries in our relationships and on some strange level enjoy the feeling of martyrdom. (Ok, just me then? I'm sure a few of you are with me. We often gain self-esteem from a need to be needed!) Wouldn't it be more sensible to seek out help, let go of the control from time to time and set boundaries so that you aren't overwhelmed by helping everyone but yourself?

I'm not suggesting complete anarchy here. I'm not very rebellious, if I'm honest. I have been well condition to follow rules and see them as supportive, rather than a hindrance, but if you always do as you 'should'; if you always please everyone else to the continual detriment of yourself, then all that will happen is you will feel resentful and duty bound. It will add to your burnout symptoms.

Doing things the way you truly want to on occasion (as long as it's legal and doesn't put anyone else in danger) is not a lot to ask yourself is it? I want to lead us on a **quiet revolution** to look out for what we need and act on it sometimes by sodding some of these 'shoulds' and I am leading the charge.

For example, if someone asked you for help and you said no, how would you feel?

What if you spent a day by yourself without your partner or kids!

You avoided a conversation with your auntie Betty about the decision you'd taken on whether to bottle or breastfeed, what might you feel like after?

You didn't volunteer for that extra event or work project when you were asked, what is MLC saying now?

You selfish cow! Really?

Isn't that what you tell yourself if you say no? I know I have. The people pleaser saboteur in me had me convinced for years that if I wasn't putting myself out for other people I was selfish. But it's different now I have clearer boundaries of 'what is OK and what is not OK' for me.

By having a clear view on when I am crossing a line in doing something to the detriment of me and my family and being able to communicate that in a loving way helps me to manage any guilt I may be feeling in saying no, the guilt is that pesky saboteur trying to convince me I 'should'. It allows the logical part of my brain to say, 'You've already volunteered for 3 hours this week, you don't have the time to do another 2 simply because someone asked, because if you do you will feel tired out and you won't get these other priorities in your life done. What you have done is good enough and the extra mile will not be good for YOU. Say no without feeling guilty."

When you are naturally giving and see it as a key part of who you are, the yes is on your lips before the person asking has finished the sentence, often the person hasn't even asked and you have waded in with support or offers or solutions. Am I right? However, like everything, it's important to be more conscious, mindful, whatever you want to call it of what you are agreeing to or how you are supporting the other person, because in the long run it makes you more giving.

But how can that be? It sounds selfish to me, you are putting yourself first. That is selfish. You've not convinced me you aren't being mean not helping. (OH yes, this is a deep seated Mean Little Cow rally this one, isn't it?)

What can you do?

You feel selfish saying no.

1. How will you feel if you say yes?

Resentful; Angry; Overwhelmed; Sanctimonious?

Why are you doing it then?

2. If you feel:

Happy; Energetic; Loving.

Go for it.

3. Would the person who asked you to do something want you to do it knowing you might burn yourself out, feel resentful, feel they owed you something?

4. Why are you feeling selfish/guilty saying no?

Give with love or don't give. Don't feel selfish or guilty.

Recently, I watched a video from Brene Brown[6] that reinforced this message. The 2 big takeaways from it were first; that 'the most compassionate people have clear boundaries'. Just like Brene, I've spent years thinking the opposite was true. Just like you, I've done lots of things for people and organisations in the past, or I've helped and supported without them asking. It has left me frazzled, sat up working at 1am in the morning, because by prioritising their needs above mine I was unable to do the things I needed for myself earlier in the day, and consequently the love in the giving was lost. The giving became exhausting, eventually resentful and duty bound. The compassion was lost. Has this ever happened to you?

However, in large part I'd said yes, or even offered support with no request or mild hints, and not communicated what the impact might be on me to the other person. How were they supposed to know?

Which brings me to the second big takeaway of the video. Brene talks about 'Giving B.I.G. - Boundaries, Integrity and Generosity.'

If you have clear boundaries and communicate them in a loving way then you are giving from a place of integrity. I take that to mean you are being honest with the person to whom you are giving, and most importantly, to yourself. By doing this you will be loving and generous in mind and action. Therefore, more loving and giving than ever before. The other part of the Mean Little Cow

---

[6] Brown, B. Retrieved from https://www.youtube.com/watch?v=ecb6ExBaW80

voice will be shouting, 'But you shouldn't give to receive and you should always put others before yourself.' These are deeply held societal and limiting beliefs that may have some truth in them, but isn't it about time you created beliefs that don't ensure that you burnout in the process of achieving them in their purest form? Can you rewrite these beliefs to live *your* truth?

Brene also talks about having boundaries in your life for those who have a negative impact on your life. It may be a friend who constantly moans and never does anything different to change her actions or behaviours. It might be a sibling, who still sees you as the 'baby' of the family and laughs at everything you are trying to do in your career. Often, over years, everyone has adopted a role and it's hard for people to adjust when you decide you don't want to play the game anymore. Brene's advice to accept that, 'they are doing the best they can right now,' is great advice. You will be able to create clear boundaries of what you are willing or unwilling to discuss with them or do for them, but you will do it from a place of love rather than getting angry or demotivated at their stand point or situation.

I know this is one area that will take a lot of work, particularly if that Mean Little Cow voice is shouting YOU are a selfish cow. But take mine and Brene's advice, give B.I.G. and know you are more loving in doing so. These feelings may also be a direct consequence contributing to your burnout, but they are a cause and a symptom, so creating boundaries is an important part of burnout recovery and staying out of it.

Another reason that overwhelm might be happening for you is actually because of underwhelm. Do you want me to repeat that?

Yes, your overwhelm could be underwhelm. I don't know about you but when I am excited and passionate about doing something I have boundless energy. The balls are flying about in the air effortlessly and I am hardly aware of them. I can work long hours and fit tonnes in with a big, fat smile on my face. Work doesn't feel like work, it's play. I am in flow. However, if my heart isn't in it or I feel I've been made to do something out of an obligation or self-imposed sense of duty, that's where the problem lies and overwhelm can kick in. I see it a lot with clients. They come with overwhelm, and as soon as they give themselves permission to remove the duty bound tasks, see the task in a different light or change the direction of their life to one that sings, the overwhelm lifts. That's because it was in fact underwhelm that was affecting them not overwhelm.

Our capacity to manage a lot is pretty phenomenal isn't it ladies? Come on be honest. However, is it doing us any good if none of that activity makes us happy or at least brings us a decent level of contentment? When we are in burnout or underwhelm it can feel like you don't like anything. Your head starts giving you lots of always and never statements, which aren't true.

The daily 'grind' or the 'relentless monotony of household tasks', as my best friend likes to refer to them, don't rock your world necessarily, but I know if I approach it with a lightness and acceptance of 'what gets done, the rest will have to wait its turn', I can enjoy the experience. Also I approach tasks in the house as a team venture. We live in the year 2016, who says mum is the cook and bottle washer? Do you really have to be superhuman and do it all for everyone?

If I had chosen to be a full time house wife then perhaps I'd come at this differently and enjoy nurturing my family and home in a different way. (I'd still ask, is it healthy for you to be on duty 24/7, 7 days a week with no breaks? That's just slave labour, isn't it?!) Who knows? Who am I to judge? But, I do know everyone in the family is making the mess and eating the food so surely everyone can do their bit? (Ok, I am judging, that's just my opinion. If none of these things leaves you resentful, or overwhelmed, ignore me it's irrelevant to you.) However, when I approach these 'tasks of doom' I try to do it with a smile on my face, and not refer to them as 'tasks of doom'. Language is everything!! LOL.

Yes, you heard right! If I approach what I see as underwhelming activity with a lightness and fun I can actually enjoy it. Blasting out your favourite 70s, 80s or 90s anthems, can make the most mundane tasks enjoyable. If I take an approach that accepts some of these tasks need to be done and if I can't outsource or delegate it then I might as well make the most of it, helps me to enjoy it more. If I insist on keeping control of it, then it's important I don't adopt a martyr attitude as I have chosen to keep hold of the task.
Can't say this always happens but I am doing my best!

Last year, I worked with a lady and one of the key issues she identified in her overwhelm was the fact that she rarely accepted the help offered by her husband. Through the coaching process, she worked on accepting the help offered, whilst not controlling the outcome and asking for help, whilst not seeing it as a weakness, but as a strength. It wasn't easy for her, but she started reaping the benefits and went for her first massage in 20 years! Might not sound much to you, but for her this was a huge leap.

These shifts don't have to be massive, but they are massively symbolic. Don't forget to breathe in the calm and clarity before you begin, five Clearing breaths.

Is your overwhelm actually underwhelm? Write your thoughts below or in your notebook.

Later we'll work out how to stop that underwhelm, by creating a vision that makes your heart sing. Once you start living that vision, whilst channelling 'Cher', 'Tina Turner' or 'Pink' etc. as you iron, do simple admin or vacuum the house, things will feel less overwhelming and more fulfilling. It sounds too simple, but it's a simple shift in our mind set that turns the pain in the task into the pleasure of getting a job done. And if you hate this stuff so much, find a way to delegate or outsource it. In Chapter 5 we'll look at how to manage ourselves to make time work for us rather than against us.

With this in mind it's good to remember that seasons are important for trees to grow and the same can be said for how we approach periods in our life. Sometimes, we just need to let leaves blow away once they've fallen, then we watch the simplicity of the tree without the leaves before we watch branches bud, then blossom, until finally, the lush foliage grows on the glorious oak tree. That's you, that is!

Chapter Five - My Own Worst Enemy

Right, this is a tough chapter because we're going to look at how, or if, you contribute to the feelings of overwhelm, anxiety, procrastination, disorganisation. As we've discussed, your environment can have a direct impact on your burnout but that isn't to say our approach and mind set can't contribute too so let's be real.

Before we begin, know that there is another chapter which celebrates the wonderful, amazing, resilient, passionate and fabulous you, but as we all have strengths and weaknesses, it is important to see where yours might be helping and hindering you.

So, don't be mean but be honest. Answer the questions below and know you'll be looking at the good stuff in a minute. Ready, steady, breathe deep 5 times before you answer.

How do you feel when you aren't at your best?

When are you most likely to see this side of you?

How does this impact on what you say do, think, and feel?

How can you reduce the likelihood of this happening?

What new habits can you develop to bring out the best of you more consistently? How will you keep up these habits? What action will you take?

Please don't let MLC take control of your head in this section. Be honest, but objective about yourself.

Right my lovely. Think you've gained some real clarity on what issues are bothering you, what habits are holding you back, what time wasters you have in your life and what brings out the worst of you? Now the fun begins as we have 'focus' we can offer some tools for you to take action.

So hold onto your seats, it might be a bumpy ride but I think you'll enjoy the path I'm about to take you down.

Section Two- Ain't no Mountain High Enough

Ok my lovely. In the last section we looked at what are the biggest issues in your life, who and what might be the biggest drain on your time, resources and energy and when the 'worst you' comes out to party.

This section is going to help you get closer to 'The Clearing'. It's going to help you fight off and train up that pesky MLC voice. It will help you use the more conscious part of the brain more often through a Solution Focused Approach to your thinking. It will help you see how and when you can bring out the best version of you more often. I hope that by the end of this section you will have made significant strides to love you more and be able to authentically celebrate that with yourself. There should be no mountain high enough, valley low enough or river wide enough to keep YOU from loving YOU! Are you ready for the climb in the woods!

You should already be able to see light through the trees, but because you've had to be constructively critical about how you contribute to the issues in your life you may still feel a bit deep in the forest. Zig Ziglar once said ""Lack of direction, not lack of time, is the problem. We all have the same twenty-four hour days." [7] This can make us feel bad about ourselves, but if used as an action signal, it can also be a wake up call to ask, 'What are we doing and why?' consciously on a regular basis.

---

[7] Ziglar, Z. Retrieved from http://www.goodreads.com/quotes/270489-lack-of-direction-not-lack-of-time-is-the-problem

"And the day came when the risk to remain tight in the bud was more painful than the risk it took to blossom."

Anais Nin

Focus is a key part of knowing what we want and how we get it. For example, if I decide I want to exercise but I focus on the immediate 'pain' of getting up and going for a run, playing on the trampoline with the treasures, or yoga or whatever I've decided, rather than focusing on the 'pleasure' I'll feel after the short term pain of having more energy or being more toned, flexible, fitter whatever my goal, it's unlikely I'll get my bum off the couch.

Equally, if I focus on the rubbish my Mean Little Cow says, rather than fight back and find proof of what is the truth. For example, if I shout at the kids it equals evidence I'm a rubbish mum. Fight back and I can provide a lot of examples of great parenting and patience, making me more able to stay patient, calm and solution focused more often than not.

We're getting clearer but we need even more focus to ensure we are able to push through short term pain for long term pleasure. This is where the real work starts, are you still in?

Chapter Six - Weather to Fly

So what are you focusing on? In Chapter 1 we focused on what issues/problems were bothering you. You asked some questions that highlighted what you'd done and what you can do to work through the issues. One of the biggest tools in my arsenal is the use of the solution focused question. If you ask a question in this way it invites positive, direct action in a way that our usual questioning doesn't. It allows us to soar mentally high above the trees and gain a different perspective and come up with creative solutions.

In his book 'Non Violent Communication' Marshall B Rosenberg states, "I find that my cultural conditioning leads me to focus attention on places where I am unlikely to get what I want. I developed NVC as a way to drain my attention... on places that have these potential to yield what I am seeking." [8] Whilst, I am no expert in NVC, I do agree that culturally we have been conditioned to approach communication and situations in a negative, aggressive way. We ask questions which attack the person they are aimed at with blame and often resentment. An example of this might be in the work place. You work in a team or manage one. You've asked for an activity to be completed and in your mind no one seemed willing or able to do it, the way you instructed. Your immediate thought might be, "Why can't these people do anything I ask? What's wrong with them?" Immediately you are in attack mode. Your thoughts are blaming them and generating feelings of anger and resentment. If you approach the team in this way, what is the likely outcome? Motivation, commitment, appreciation? Unlikely. So why do we approach the situation this way?

---

[8] Rosenburg, M.B. (2003) Nonviolent Communication: A Language in Life. USA. PuddleDancer Press.p4.

[I discuss the concept of Solution Focused Thinking and how we have default thinking i.e. the way we've been conditioned to think as stated above, which largely comes from our survivor brain or we have supportive thinking that can be supercharged by Solution Focused thinking. This thinking supports our Sage, Logical, Conscious side of the brain. Sign up for my FREE e-book on my website[9] for further activities on training yourself to adopt this type of thinking more often. It's the type of thinking that helped me get this book out, despite massive resistance from my default thinking.]

First, I would look at the questions I'm asking. Is it true that it's *always* that way? I'm sure you could find examples of good work for all of them at one time or another. Second, you are taking no responsibility for your actions or feelings in this statement. You are asking what is wrong with them but could you have given the instructions in a different way, which may have helped them understand what needed to be done? Are you approachable enough, that if they don't understand, or are struggling, they can come to you for additional support? Again, careful MLC doesn't creep in here and start making you doubt yourself, but be honest and truthful to yourself in a kind, loving and supportive way.

Third, it's time to start thinking in a solution focused way, ask the question to take responsibility for your feelings and to take positive action to getting what you need out of the situation. In this example, you might have asked, "What do I need to do next, to ensure the team are motivated, working independently and clear on how to achieve the task I've set them? What additional support can I offer? Can you see the difference? If you come at the question in this way

---

[9] Leyland, M. (2015) Retrieved from www.woodforthetreescoaching.co.uk

you'll come up with actions you need to take to make it happen in a more positive and enjoyable way.

So with this in mind, think of your top 5 issues/problems. Think how you usually think about them. Burnout is a breeding ground for default thinking at its best. Is this questioning helping or hindering you?

Ask the question in a solution focused way and then underneath each one add a list of actions you can start to take from today. However, before you do that let's do those important Clearing breaths!

Default attacking thoughts:

1.
2.
3.
4.
5.

Solution Focused Questions:

1.
2.
3.
4.
5.

Actions:	By when:	By who?

Don't know about you but I'm feeling lighter already!

Chapter Seven - Eye of the Tiger

Ok, there's one thing that's probably still going to keeping you stuck and stopping you from bouncing back from burnout.

Guess what it is?

Yep, sorry to upset you but it's YOU! Your fears of making change will continue to feed any self-doubt you have and sabotage your efforts to make changes that will help you thrive, not strive.

Recently I asked an online network of women to share the thing that holds them back the most. I expected to hear general things like overwhelm, motivation, procrastination, self-doubt etc. etc.

The overriding issue that held them all back was fear.

I don't know why that surprised me, but it did. It shouldn't have, as at the root of all the issues I've mentioned above is fear. Overwhelm is a fear of there being so much going on that you can't cope and you may just fall over in the process of trying.

Procrastination is a fear of failure, or often success as you are scared of what taking action will bring.

Self-doubt is the fear that you are not good enough or not deserving enough of what it is you are aiming for or trying to achieve.

Fear is your trees. It's the dark, enclosing feeling of being lost, frightened and unsure how to get out. Well, sod that. You *are* good enough and you can get to a place where you can see the trees for what they are. How do I know? I've done it, and if I can do it, so can you! But you have to put up a bit of a fight for this one, in a positive way of course.

Now, if you are being positive you could say she is looking after you. She is protecting you from taking dangerous risks or feeling uncomfortable. She's sometimes shining a light on the areas of your life that might need changing or improving. This is all fine if you can listen to her, accept that which has truth in it, take action and leave it at that. Unfortunately, as I've mentioned before "Mean

Little Cow" is also conditioned through many references and limiting beliefs set from childhood to exaggerate and be aggressive. The more we listen and don't act, the louder and more obnoxious she'll get.

If you are feeling you aren't making progress in a certain area or making some mistakes, left to "Mean Little Cow's" devices you will end up the worst and most rubbish at what she is telling you. If you believe her!

The way to keep your "MLC" under control is to listen and act. Pop over to my blog later and read more [10]

As women we seem to expect we can do it all and have it all, after all that's what we were brought up thinking. Consequently, we feel like failures when there is a cost or sacrifice to having a lot in one area. E.g. if we have kids and a great career, we might feel we sacrifice time with the kids. If we have more time with the kids, we might feel we have to sacrifice part of our career. Often, it leaves us feeling lacking and guilty, which feeds our MLC even more.

Well, no more!! I don't believe we can have it all (in one go) something has to give! If we burn ourselves out trying to do it all, be it all and have it all our "MLCs" can really get their teeth in and

---

[10] Leyland, M. (2015) Retrieved from http://www.woodforthetreescoaching.co.uk/blog/5-simple-steps-to-be-your-own-best-friend-forever

have us believing we are doing nothing well. It's a lie! So, from now on we are fighting back! Box it off! If "MLC" starts to give it large, give it back. Be your Own Best Friend. Would you let your BF be talked to the way you are talking to you?

First things first, breathe. Clear your mind of any chit chat about in there. Concentrate on your breath.

First ask if it's true?

If it's not all true, what is and what isn't? What can you do to improve what is true? E.g. if it's true you've shouted at your husband/partner and told her/him (s) he's a complete #@$%, what can you do to repair the damage? What can you do to ensure you don't get to that level of insult in your communication in the future? What proof can you find that you are a good enough partner who loves and nurtures your relationship?

Use the 'Box Off' chart to find examples.

MLC	Truth	Action Signal

More often than not you'll prove the "MLC" wrong. Be your own best friend. However, if you believe the "MLC" is completely true and you are a "rubbish" partner and have issues of violent communication then use the information for good.

Decide today is the day it's going to change. Read Marshall. B. Rosenberg's book!

Use solution focused questioning and ask, "How can I improve my communication and relationship to find love, peace and acceptance with my partner?"

Instead of beating yourself with a big, fat self-doubt, I'm s$%t stick!! Make the change you want to be! It won't be easy and you will fall off the wagon, but you'll be trying and working towards a bigger, better more bubbly you.

Using the technique above for any feelings of self-doubt to beat off your "MLC" will help you take away the risks your "MLC" is fearful of. By being kind to yourself and working on learning from the fear and what it is trying to tell you, you will grow stronger, more in control and more able to know the truth and the lies "MLC" tells.

Just to add, if the negativity is coming from someone else and it starts your "MLC" spouting its nonsense the same applies. I've had clients who've had partners who feed the "MLC" with their limiting beliefs, family, friends or colleagues. When this happens again ask the question "is it true?" and work through the Box Off Sheet. Also remember what we looked at in terms of boundaries in Chapter 4.

Another situation when "MLC" rears her head is if you make a mistake, oh she can get vicious then, particularly if you have perfectionist or people pleasing tendencies.

How do you counteract the "MLC" saying you are a disaster, a fraud, rubbish, a phoney, whatever she is saying? You've made a mistake. Fine. How can you learn from it to gain strength for the future? If it's not possible to undo the mistake or repair the damage you can reassure "MLC" that you won't make the same mistake again. Above all find examples of when you've done a great job! Prove that "MLC" wrong by being your own 'BFF'. If you don't love you and blow your own trumpet, then who the hell will?

I've watched clients who have been barraged daily by their "MLC" voice gain complete control over it. They have used its initial spouting to take conscious action or to calm it by explaining that there is no imminent danger and that the action they are about to take, whilst uncomfortable and challenging, is for the long term good.

This has enabled them to live fuller lives with exciting achievements and self-care that "MLC" would never have let them attempt before such as starting up a business; taking a business from a local to a national level; having a full weekend away from their husband and children to meet a friend, guilt free!

In burnout MLC can run the show and bring you down. It's essential you take control of her as you start making positive changes to your environmental situation.

Chapter Eight - It's a Beautiful Day

In Chapter 3, you took a good long look at the habits and routines that weren't giving you the life you want and deserve. This chapter is a chance to put that right, but I warn you now it's simple but not easy.

I find it so interesting as humans how we can quickly adopt a "bad" habit. For example, I hadn't been on Facebook since 2012. I'd decided it was feeding my feelings of guilt. It was when Facebook was relatively new and as I gained 'friends' I felt It was necessary to 'actually' communicate with them, send personal messages that had some weight to and actually, really care about whether they replied. So because I couldn't keep up with it all and it added to the overwhelm I was feeling with work/life I decided to delete my account.

Fast forward to today and Facebook is a different animal. I do post things I think family and friends will like and occasionally comment on their feeds but I use it more to connect with likeminded women around the world who are on a similar business journey to me. Hence, it's addictive. Very quickly this habit of picking up my phone as I wake and checking my inbox for comments before I sleep has wheedled its way into my daily routine. Consequently, I could watch 20 mins of time that I could be sending out emails, making a call or actually, truly listening to my daughter sat right in front of me!

There are lots of little rituals and routines that cause us to procrastinate, stay stuck and waste time that could otherwise be productive. For you it might be a 2 hour soap fest each night (that used to be one of mine but doing the girls' bath and bedtime story then got me out of it). It might be going to bed ridiculously late in a bid to get 'me time' but then leaving you shattered, fractious and sluggish the next day.

In the last chapter you identified what those habits were so now I want you to use a solution focused approach to work out what you'd like to see change and how you are going to make it happen.

For example, you may have written down you have an inconsistent bedtime routine with your children that allows them to stay up late and means you have no space in the day to just 'be', work on your business, or do the small tasks like sort out the clothes for the next day to get the morning off to a good start.

First, don't beat yourself up!! MLC might start in here "Oooh you time waster" "Can't even get your kids to bed" Blah, Blah, Blah. Moo, moo…. Trot on!

Listen to what truth there is and then ask the solution focused question that will help you take action and want to stick to it. An example would be:

What do I want the evening to look and feel like?

How do I bring in small changes over a period of time that will bring about a calmer, more structured routine?

What resistance may I get from X, Y or Z?

How will I combat this resistance?

How do I get them to 'buy into' the changes I want to make?

How do I do this in a loving manner that doesn't come from a blame and attacking standpoint?

How can I get them to contribute to which changes need to happen?

How will this change impact on me? The family?

How will the family and I benefit?

Once I establish this improved routine, what can I do to enjoy the time it will give me?

At first this feels so strange. We are not brought up to think like this. I know sometimes I feel a bit 'Stepford Wife' about it and think, is it really possible to think like this all the time? Honestly, probably not and that question itself is in a negative voice! But what I do know, and what I am positive about, is that when I, or my clients, do mindfully engage with an issue in this way, amazing things happen.

When you communicate from a place of love with the family the results are so much more productive than from asking in a tired, attacking way. By asking the question in this solution focused way it demands positive action and change. It gives your thoughts a higher positive energy, those who delve into the manifestation world might say a higher vibrational energy.

The second part of this equation is the need to be committed to maintaining the action needed to have lasting change. We've all been there. Two weeks into a diet or exercise regime we start to lose momentum and then eventually give up. How many times have you paid out gym subs **to just not go**?

Once I watched a leading sports coach, turned business coach, called Todd Herman explaining how we are either "Ow" or "Wow" people. [11]What I think he meant was that we either were motivated by pleasure or by pain? You know what I mean. If something starts to give us serious pain we are motivated to change it, alternatively if we can feel motivated to change something or embrace something new we will do it or if we can feel the pleasure that would be gained by achieving X, Y and Z before we even start making the changes then that would be the driving force to get us there.

Think about it.

---

[11] Herman, T. & Forleo, M. (2014) Retrieved through https://www.youtube.com/watch?v=CKLK04IU4Do

How many people finally lose a significant amount of weight *only* when they are told they can't have an operation to save their life, *unless* they lose the weight? This is an 'Ow' brain mentality. It's a person who is being driven largely by their sub conscious and default thinking and pain as a driver.

However, a person who quits smoking because they wake up one morning and realise that if they didn't smoke they would be financially better off, that their health and wellbeing would be improved and that it would make them feel good about themselves to have kicked the habit, will simply put down the cigarettes and not smoke again. This person is led more by the 'WOW' brain mentality. They are being guided by their conscious or supportive,
'Sage' brain.

Both of these examples are extremes, but it is good to identify if your actions are led by pain or pleasure and whether you are motivated by pain or pleasure.

Tony Robbins also emphasises this in much of his teaching. He also explains how we need 3 things to make a lasting change. Focus, Strategy and Inner Control [12](it's the point of inner control where pain and pleasure come in). Focus is when we are identifying the goals and change that we want to bring about. Here we get a clear intention to do it. But sadly, that's not enough. How many times have you written goals or to do lists that just haven't translated into action?

Well, again don't beat yourself up it might be you didn't have a Strategy. Strategy, in this case is the tools and information needed to put the focus into practise. For example, you know you want to wear that bikini on the beach with confidence so for you that would mean toning up a few areas or perhaps just getting a mind-

---

[12]   Robbins,   T.   (2013)   Retrieved   through
https://www.youtube.com/watch?v=4JIzngH9UBQ

set that accepted what you've got and not caring what anyone else thinks. If it was the former you might look at exercise plans, sign up for a gym class, go on YouTube or buy a DVD to exercise at home, buy a rowing machine for the bedroom. All of these are 'strategy' based actions they now demonstrate 'motivation'. But sorry to be the bearer of bad news but we aren't there yet, because we now need commitment.

Lasting commitment and this is where the battle between pain and pleasure comes in. This is where Mr Robbins 'inner control' plays a major role. Inner control is you taking consistent action. You taking daily action that takes you closer and closer to the end goal. Now this sounds so easy on paper but it doesn't take into account our self-limiting beliefs.

 "You don't deserve to be that shape because you are a lazy, lump. Who'd love you?"

 "You don't need to get that education because you aren't clever enough to use it."

"You shouldn't be setting up a business, what do you know about accounts and marketing?"

 When our MLC kicks in with these self-limiting beliefs start, that's when you need your 'inner control' to kick in. It might be you start to sabotage yourself through fear of failure, or success. So, now you are aware of what it is going to take to maintain the changes you'd like in your life you need to decide what routines and rituals would help you live life more fully, with more energy, with more passion and more contentment.

Also look at if you are coming at the issue with the 'Ow' or 'Wow' brain because you can then work with this.

Right let's get clear and breathe. Concentrate on your breath. Clear your mind. Let's begin.

So using a solution focused approach look at the issues. Decide what question you want to ask yourself and then decide on the action to be taken.

Issue1	
Solution Focused Question	
Action	

Issue 2	
Solution Focused Question	
Action	

Issue 3	
Solution Focused Question	
Action	

Now you know what you want to do, you've got your focus. What 'Strategy' do you need to employ?

Using 'triggers' throughout the day on a consistent and daily basis can help to bring about and maintain new habits. So what can you do to set up these triggers on your phone or in a visual aid that you would see regularly throughout the day?

How will this help you to do what you want to do? How can you recommit to the why when this trigger signals an action you need to take to make the change/improvement?

Focus	Strategy
Goal: To tone abdominal muscles. **Actions:** Buy a Pilates machine and do one hour work outs 4 times per week.	Set time in the diary and trigger the reason I want to do it in my phone with an affirmation. E.g. I will have a toned tummy that makes me happy in my own skin

Hurrah, we've now got focus and strategy but we need a bit of inner control. I know you won't be able to pre-empt them all but

write down the barriers you are likely to face in achieving the above actions using the strategy you've decided to adopt. Again, be honest here the only person you are kidding is you. So if you know as in the example above that you'll start to procrastinate or eat for comfort write it down. Think about the issues you've identified and the barriers you have to face. Don't forget your
Clearing breaths.

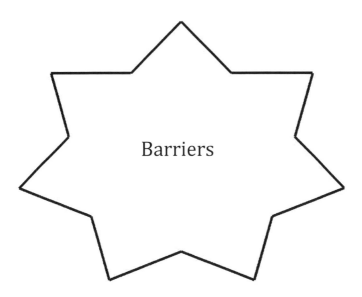

Again, you know what most of the barriers are so what solutions can you come up with to overcome them?

For example, if you are driven by pain but the pleasure of achieving the goal itself isn't enough reward, what additional rewards can you give yourself to make that little bit of pain or discomfort pleasurable? Get it? Sometimes you've got to go over, round or simply head butt through the barrier to get to the other side. Looking at it from a number of perspectives is always helpful, not easy if you are in the middle of burnout to be fair but definitely the way to get out of that situation. So, breathe and think, in that order.

Chapter Nine- What have you done today to make you feel proud?

Ok, we had to dig a bit deeper there to see what we can do to bring routines that help us into our day and how the pain of making that change can become the pleasure. In Chapter 5 you had a good look at 'worst me' and when she comes out the most.

I love this chapter because it allows you to celebrate the beautiful, dynamic and amazing person you are! Its part of my favourite activity I do with clients who have issues of self-doubt or lack confidence.

So, go on. Take a good, hard look at yourself and tell me all there is to love about you. Be loud, be proud and enjoy luxuriating in the wonder that is YOU.

Before you start, breathe. Clear your mind. Concentrate on your breath and then on YOU.

First, sit with each question for a minute and have a good think. Now, answer these questions:

How do you feel when you are at your best?

When are you most likely to see 'best me'?

How does this impact on what you say? Do? Think? Feel?

How can you increase the likelihood of 'best me' appearing?

What new habits can you develop to bring out the best of you?

What action will you take?

It is important that we focus on what we do well. A little part of my night time ritual feeds the self-acceptance in me. In a lovely little notebook, bought by a good friend, I note down at least 3 of the things I'm grateful for and 3 things I'm proud of myself for, for that day. I've also got it on the daily planner I use. "What have you done today to make you feel proud?" Sometimes I love me so much I fill out both! How very un-British of me!!!

Allow you to get stuck into the exercise and enjoy it. Tell us all your best bits and don't miss out any detail. You know how good you are. You do. You may have been burying it deep inside, under the dirty washing or in a pile of papers, or allowing the 'Mean Little Cow' voice to drown out all the good stuff and focus on the little mistakes or weaknesses that everyone deals with every day, but it is there.

Use lots of I am ….. Statements and I have…..comments to build a great picture of you. Surround this tree with words of love. She is YOU, she is.

For example:

I am strong. I am resilient. I am determined. I am clever. I am funny. I am gentle. I am caring. I am compassionate. I have a good heart. I have great values. I am alive. I am a wonderful friend, mother, daughter, carer, and wife. I am me. I am enough.

I don't know why we find this so difficult. I have watched women's toes literally curl as they have had to express something good about themselves.

Perhaps, as it is here in the UK, it's a cultural thing of not wanting to appear big headed. For some it's from a family system that said, 'you shouldn't get above your station' or 'blow your own trumpet'.

Whatever it is for you forget about it. It may have been a 'friend' at school who put you down to build up her self-esteem.

Really, just forget that you were ever condition to believe these things for the purpose of this exercise. If right here, right now you can't celebrate all that is great about YOU, where else can you. If you are really stuck, put yourself in the shoes of someone who loves you and write what you think they would say about you. Eventually I want you to give yourself that validation and acceptance and not need it from others. However, if that is the *only way* you can complete this exercise now, think how would my best friend, my colleagues (co-workers) or parents etc. describe me.

Enjoy yourself. Enjoy YOU.

Now, you are going to use what you doodled above to write yourself a love letter. Imagine that you are the greatest love of your life (You should be). Tell yourself how, why, when and what you love about YOU. It might feel a bit daft, but believe me after years of your "MLC" putting the boot in; you could do with a bit of cheerleading.

If this affirmation and validation of how fabulous you are comes externally you won't believe it in times of stress, you'll doubt it and worst of all you'll need it to feel good about you. Write this letter to yourself and refer to it whenever you doubt yourself or if someone else knocks your confidence. Being able to love yourself is vital to strong self-esteem. It's essential to personal confidence. It's critical to a long lasting love of you, warts and all. Yes. You have warts. We all do, but here we don't need to highlight them. Here we are going to emphasise all the positives and see where your negatives are strengths.

Get a beautiful pen; if you like get some beautiful scented paper. You are worth it! Sit in a comfortable seat and let your words of love cascade over you in a way you've never let yourself do it before. Think of different scenarios, with different people and different events when you have excelled, or at least been good enough in your head if that's as far as you can get today. Think of the little things, holding a door for a stranger; smiling at someone when they are sad; pitching a great idea to your team in work; enjoying a conversation with your teenage son/daughter; a friend.

You are a wonderful woman.

Let's hear all about it.

"What is my greatest gift?"

Michala Leyland

Love letter to myself Dear

Me (or insert name),

I am writing this letter of love to let you know I love you because...

Love you forever,

Me (or Insert name) xxxxx

Section Three- Dream a little dream of me.

Three of the most marvellous, magical tools I have to share with you in this last section of a vision, a mission and a success definition have made such a dramatic impact on what I do and how I live my life, and that of my clients' lives.

In a way, the fact we don't do this earlier in our lives is a real shame it's what contributes to our burnout as we negotiate environments that don't meet our values, needs and personalities, however, if you've picked up this book in your 20's, hurray!!! Doing this work could save you years of wondering what the *hell* am I doing and why? LOL.

Saying that, all experience brings lessons, learning and growth so perhaps it's only as we get older we can truly understand what we need and want at the same time, although I'm met some very self-aware and emotionally resilient 20 year olds, so as ever best not to generalise .

So, I start with my favourite question;

What are you doing and why? No, really, think about it deeply.

Having asked this at workshops I run for women, just like you, I had reactions as dramatic as sharp, horrified intakes of breath to nervous giggles in order to avoid going deep into this thought.

Why?

I think it's because we really don't ask it at its deepest level very often, if ever, and if we do we are scared that our lives are so far from the answer we fear what that means.

What makes you run around like a headless chicken?

What makes you so busy, busy, busy? What exactly are you doing?

What makes you work so hard and it's never enough? Eat such rubbish it makes you fat, unhealthy and unsatisfied but comforts you? Spend so much money on things you can't afford and only brings instant gratification? Give no time to yourself in order to feel like a great mum, wife, and employee?

Think.

What are you running around for and is it really necessary? At one point I had my children on such a gruelling schedule of activities that it wasn't doing them any good. It definitely wasn't doing me any good! I thought I was helping to stimulate them, help them grow mentally and emotionally, but actually, I was exhausting my introverted daughter and tiring myself out in the process.

Consequently, I thought it through and dropped several of the activities we were involved with that were at times when the girls would have been better off having quiet time at home, and a chance to actually play with the huge amount of toys we have in the house! Sound familiar to you?

Are you spending lots of money that you don't have, on material things? What is making you do that? Is there another way of getting that pleasurable feeling of making a purchase without putting yourself in the pain of debt? Could you get that pleasure from volunteering in a hospice or looking after an elderly neighbour? Would that feed your self-esteem more than a beautiful pair of shoes and nice handbag?

Are you filling a deep need in you with *things*? I'm not saying this is the case and there is no judgement on my part (I love shoes!) but it's important to be clear on what is driving us.

Are you eating out of comfort a lot of the time? Out of boredom? Is there a way of getting those needs filled in different ways than eating food that is neither nourishing nor helping give you energy to live the fun-filled life you want? If you are bored, what can you do to fill your time more energetically? If you need comfort, can you find activities or spend time with people who make you feel good about life?

Are you putting in ridiculous hours at work because if you don't, you feel you aren't good enough? If you don't put in hour after extra hour, you are letting the team down? Are you exhausting yourself so that you can feel like you are enough?

I repeat the all-important question, what are you doing and why are you doing it?

Think deeply.

Now, if things aren't how you'd like, ask this, what do you want to be doing and why? What can you imagine doing and how would it make you feel to do it more often? What have you got already that you want to maintain or develop? How will this impact on what you do and how you feel?

Before we move on I want you to know that it is as important to enjoy what you have right this minute, as it is to grow and develop. Being grateful for the here and now doesn't have to make you complacent, yet also it doesn't have to make you dissatisfied with everything around you. It feels like a contradiction sometimes but even in the worst case scenario people find light.

If things are as you'd like but there is room for growth ask, "How can I get more of X, Y, Z into my life in order that I enjoy my life to the full?" Note: I didn't say happier. Happier all the time is fool's gold in my opinion. Yes, we want to feel happier the majority of the time but we have to feel all emotions, it's what make us human.

It's worth spending time considering what you define as happy at this point too. Is it constant excitement or a general contentment? Is it a mix of both? If you can gain clarity on this it will also influence your vision for now and the future.

Chapter Ten - Visions

This vision, these dreams, are to help us bring more of what we cherish or more of what we know we need into our lives, but I am a strong believer in gratitude. If we show and have gratitude for what we have in our lives already, we will be grateful for anything we achieve in the future.

If we strive forward without appreciating what we have in the here and now we may find when we get what we think we want, we look back and have been miserable for years pursuing it. Plus have you ever achieved something and it hasn't brought you the feeling you thought it would? Imagine not enjoying all the time pursuing that dream to be disappointed in the result. Why would you do that? You need to enjoy the journey as much as the destination. This, like many so called clichés, is so true.

Before you start out ask this Solution Focused Question, 'What will you enjoy on the road to achieving this vision?'

First things first, you know the drill let's breathe. Clear your mind of anything whirling about in there. Concentrate on your breath.

If you've never done a Vision Board before, you are in for a treat and I highly recommend you do it. You can do it electronically on Pinterest or in a PowerPoint, or you can do what I love to do and embrace your inner child. Find the scissors, glue, mags, newspapers, pictures from that t'interweb to make a great, big, dream drenched collage.

I did mine with my youngest daughter, who also did her own. It was a wonderful afternoon. She loved it and I loved it. I loved seeing the pictures of very cute puppies she had cut out to try to convince me we should have a dog. Good try!! Hey don't judge me. Her dream will come true, when she gets her own home! Or when

I'm happy to prioritise dog walking into my day, whichever comes quickest.

You'll need A1/A3 piece of paper or card (One client did it on wallpaper lining paper, another on a cork board; don't let a lack of materials keep you stuck. Use what you have!) You can use pictures; words; felt tip pens; glitter glue; gel pens; whatever rocks your world.

Above all dream big. If you had no time, finance, mean little cow voices, family or work commitments constraining you what would your life look like? How would it be?

An exercise I do with clients to help them get clear is to write down in detail what they would love to be saying to someone they've not seen since school, at a school reunion in 5 years' time. Take each area of your life that is important to you and write in detail what you'd like to be saying. Include all the things you are most grateful for now and expand that. This can help you gain the insights for the images you will put on your vision board.

Think about whether you want a 5 year, 10 year or life time Vision Board as this will make all the difference. My daughter did a 5 year one. I did a 10 year one for my life and another 5 year one for my Business but there are no rules. Be creative, let your imagination run riot.

Equally, if you are struggling with what you want it can be good to think about the opposite of what you want at this stage. What don't you want to feel like, be doing or saying in 5 years/10 years' time? If you are more 'Ow' brain, really feel the pain of it and use it to motivate you to make the changes you are dreaming now.

It doesn't matter how farfetched it feels. What your vision will bring you is a sense of what makes you happy, motivated, energetic, inspired, joyful or giddy, probably a bit scared if it's really big. Oh my giddy aunt, how am I going to do that? How am I going to have that in my life? Let's face it, if you achieve even 70% of what you put on that board you'll be in a better place than if you've given it no thought and not spent your days living your actual dreams.

Equally it doesn't matter if it's not a big dream if it's filled with little things that would bring you joy and contentment. It's your vision. I've had clients who have come to me who have come out of a burnout and the idea of big dreams and goals feels too pressured, too overwhelming in its self. They don't want huge amounts of materials things or adventures at this point in the road. They want inner peace and to enjoy being present with their partner and children, they want time to spend with their ageing granny. They want simplicity. In this 24 hour, choice driven world we live in it can be one of the hardest things to achieve.

The beauty of this vision is that by seeing something visual it will be a powerful motivator. It will be a daily reminder of what you want in your life and what you love now. It will make what you want clear and focused. It will remind you on difficult days what, why and how you are taking the action and making the effort to make these things happen in your life. It will help you bring a bit of that vision, even if it's a currently diluted version, into your life daily.

An example of this is that I would like my children to experience some of the adventures my husband and I had in our early 30s. Whilst we are pursuing our dream of creating a warm, friendly family home, having bought a house that needs everything doing to it, we have only planned one major trip next year. In the meantime we are creating adventure through weekly bike rides through the woods, taking the children to climb trees or having a go in a dinghy down by the sea or all body boarding. We create shell and pebble pictures in the sand and sledge down massive sand dunes. Day trips to Go Ape, or our local Climbing Hangar, are experiences that feed that need for adventure along the way. It gives us a small 'buzz' and ensures we enjoy the time in-between when we are able to go on our exciting American Road trip where we'll sleep with the danger of live bears under a canopy of stars.

Is what you currently do in your vision or are there positive action steps needed to take you in a different direction? Does this excite you? Is there an opportunity in your burnout that you didn't see before to improve in your current environment or is it time to change it?

So, dream big, or simply, my lovely and use the vision to have the weeks, months, years YOU want to live by understanding what makes your heart sing. I'd love you to share your Vision Boards with me over on my Facebook page (www.facebook.com/woodforthetreescoaching) once you've completed them.

Chapter Eleven - The Power

So, gorgeous girl. Now I want to share with you the secret of how I achieve my vision with joy in my heart and fire in my belly. I have a purpose that is married to my passion. I have created a 'Mission Statement' for my life.

Well, if it's good enough for companies, it's good enough for YOU and I'll show you why.

Your Mission Statement is a statement you can say to yourself every single day. It's a statement you can call on if an opportunity presents itself to check if it's for you or if you can comfortably and confidently say no. It's a statement that will give you energy when the daily drudge of washing, cleaning, and thinking of everyone else in the family gets the better of the way you are coming at your day. It's a statement that can capture your values and create a confident belief in YOU and how you want to live your life.

At first it might seem a bit of an odd idea. After all aren't Mission Statements for companies and organisations. Well, if you read my blog, "Are you the CEO or Managing Partner of Your Family?" [13]You'll know that I think some of the principles of business, when applied to the home, can be really effective.

Are you up for it? Let's give it a go and see what you come up with. Like anything you read in a personal development book, it's not until you do the work will you know if it will work for YOU.

First things first, breathe. Clear your mind of anything whirling about in there. Concentrate on your breath. And we'll begin.

---

[13]   Michala   Leyland   (2015)   Retrieved   through http://www.woodforthetreescoaching.co.uk/blog/are-you-the-ceo-in-your-home-top-tips-for-more-productivity-and

Think about what you would like in your life. You'll have a pretty good idea by now if you've done the work in the previous chapters, especially in the Vision chapter.

What would you like to do for yourself or others?

What would like to give to yourself or others?

How would you like to feel on a regular basis?

This is very personal to you but I'll share my Mission Statement so you can get a feel for how it can look.

"I, Michala Leyland, know, see, hear, and feel that my life's purpose is to lead a full life with my family surrounded by love, whilst supporting people to make positive changes."

Michala Leyland

You can see from my Mission this is how I want to live my life. I feel it. I see it. I know it to be true. It's simple. It's flippin' powerful!! It helps me stay strong. It helps keep me on track. It allows me to weather emotional stresses and strains knowing its ok, part of life and that I still have my mission and so much to be grateful for in my life.

This, coupled with a clear definition of success, keeps me at the top of my mental game and thus I take action, daily and make things happen the way I want to in a way that suits me. I have freedom in this knowledge and understanding of what my life means. Freedom from the 'Mean Little Cow's' hold on me and her unhelpful comments and lies (or at least allows me to question what the fear laden cow is saying, and take action despite it).

Remember: don't make it too complicated or wordy. This is something you want to use as an affirmation or as a reminder when the chips are down. You need to remember it and it mean something to you, no one else. So you might look at my mission statement and think, that's not what I'd write, or that seems very uninspiring. Well it doesn't have to inspire anyone else but me, so it doesn't matter what you take from it. Same as if you write a mission that only you find motivating. It only needs to motivate you because it's YOURS.

In the space below get some ideas and key words down. What's important to you?

Love, Contribution, Security, Adventure, Success??

Having a Vision and Mission Statement has given me the courage to develop On Line Programmes such as The Clearing On Line or The Solution Focused Sisterhood Membership Club.
It has enabled me to write this book (and two smaller e-books) and publish them. It's given me the strength to make personal

changes in my routines and communication with family and friends. It's allowed me to say yes to a 'modelling' opportunity, sing in front of an audience, abseil a building, Periscope daily, win

'On Line Bizmum of the Year 2015', despite only starting a Facebook page in January 2015 and joining Twitter in April 2015, Periscope in May and my own Blab show co-hosted with Jai Garcia @GetSelfbelief by April 2016!

It's a cherry on your cake my lovely and I want you to have a Vision and a Mission and to live by them.

Use the box below, or get a lovely sheet of paper, to write a Mission Statement that makes your soul sing, puts fire in your belly and warms the cockles of your heart.

My Beautiful Mission

Can you feel it?

Shout it out!

Scream it at the top of your lungs!

Sing it.

Taste it.

Love it!!!

It's yours. Own that mission.

'Work it baby! Work it!' (Love a bit of Pretty Woman don't you?! LOL)

Print it out. Put it on your fridge, in a frame, in your diary, on your sun visor in the car, next to your bed.

Put it in your sight. Get it on your Vision Board.

You've got a Mission and a Vision what are you waiting for? Go out there and enjoy the life you want. The life you love. The life you flippin' well deserve. This is bouncing back from burnout. This is why burnout can be a joy! It's a chance to reassess and redesign how you want life to be.

But before you start taking action you've one thing missing.

A definition of Success that works for you. Let's get cracking.

Success.

What do you see when you think of this word?

Is it money? For most people it is lots of money. Having a work life that brings lots of money is seen as success in western culture.

What about status?

If you are the CEO of a company or you have worked your way into the Senior Management team of an organisation this too is seen as success.

What about Power?

Being the Head of State or a politician in a country is seen as a successful position to have.

However, what if that money had come at the expense of children in poverty, would that money seem so successful?

What if that CEO was actually battling panic attacks everyday under the strain of maintaining that successful position? Would that be seen as success?

What if that power had been handed to that politician because of their parents' standing in the local community not on their own merit? Would that be seen as success?

On the surface of it success has been painted to be all these things in western culture, but if you dig to find out the cost that some people have paid for that success, you might start to think that success isn't as easily defined as we have been led to believe. Now don't get me wrong I'm not saying money, power or status are bad things. Great things can be achieved with all three; however, rarely do we look at the price 'some' people pay for the 'perceived' successes. It is simply a given in our society.

I'm on a real mission with this 'Success' thing, because I believe that part of the reason I burnt out all those years ago is because I was chasing a version of success that I'd been spoon fed from birth, but that didn't nourish me at a value level.

All that striving to achieve the next promotion, for more money and to be more in control was the road to overwhelm for me because it wasn't feeding me internally.

All of the external indicators of success mentioned above weren't giving me the internal success my body was craving.

Do you know what I mean?

I've had clients express this to me, that they achieved the promotion but felt like a fraud. They didn't enjoy the 'success' of it, because they felt they had had to work even harder to justify their position, before anyone catches them out (a common sabotaging behaviour of 'Hyper Achievers' by the way, according to Shirzad Chamine[14]).

There are others who had a remarkable income, by anyone's standards, but they found that the work that they were doing was soulless and unrewarding, or they were working so hard that they had no time to spend the money on adventures they'd been endeavouring to purchase.

They had achieved a level of Power within their position, but found that the media scrutiny and personal invasion into their lives was too much.

Therefore, I believe it is critical to find out what success actually means to you at your core before you begin to set goals to achieve

---

[14] Chamine, S. (2015) Positive Intelligence. P18

it. If success is centred on material gain and position you may never be satisfied until the point at which you achieve it (and even then it is likely you'll keep striving towards the next goal as you find achieving the previous one wasn't as fulfilling as you hoped.)

Once you have a success definition you can refer to it to make important decisions. A client I worked with recently, had the opportunity of a promotion. Previously she admitted she would have just gone for the position because she felt like she 'should', that she would be a failure somehow if she didn't. By referring to her success definition, and looking at all the advantages and disadvantages of taking or not taking the promotion, she walked away from the session confident and assured that that opportunity wasn't right for her at this time. It didn't align with her definition of success, that she'd worked on with me, and it would open up opportunities in the future to experiences that would give her a stronger feeling of success and self-satisfaction.

Isn't it about time, your loveliness, that you created a definition of success that will work for YOU and allow YOU to feel happy throughout the journey, not just once you've achieved the end results?

Let's do this then!! Don't forget to breathe first!

Right, I want you to write down what you feel success feels like to you?

If that first attempt was very outcome focused. E.g. I'd like a Porsche; to travel all over the world; to run a multi-million pound business; to raise a happy child.

Go inside. Get excited by the thought of it. Get clear on what it means at your core. These are the internal feelings you have when you feel success remember NOT things/goals. If you went there first time maybe look at the outcomes now and see if they really line up with your core feelings.

*What does success **feel** like to you?*

Now, at some point we all fear success. Perhaps our experience of 'success' has been the one we were conditioned with since birth and it hasn't been positive. Perhaps success is so pinned on financial gain, status and power you've never achieved success in your eyes because there is always someone to compare your 'successes' against and you feel like you fall short. Comparisonitis only feeds 'Mean Little Cow' and we don't want that!

Don't get me wrong I'm not saying that achieving money, status or power are wrong in themselves, we need strong leaders and money is a fact of life and can be used to do lots of great things for you and others. However, if these are the benchmarks we build our definition of success on, we may never feel successful, despite having success, because we have pinned our definition on the external. Perhaps you fear success because 'Mean Little Cow' tells you you can't handle it. She'll definitely be telling you that if you've had a burnout. Am I right?

You fear success because you believe it will take time away from those you love. You fear success because those around you will think you are 'above your station' and not want to be with you anymore. You fear success because you believe that it will burn you out. Whatever your subconscious fear, it's a limiting belief that will keep you stuck and unable to achieve the success you desire. They are merely stories we tell ourselves, which are shaped from references that were pretty much set from early childhood. Therefore, they are often not your beliefs but those of people who were significant in your life.

As ever whether it's "Mean Little Cow" or a straightforward fear or belief, I am a big believer in listening to it. It's got a valid place in your life and it is trying to protect you from death or mortal danger. Listen too long and you will stay stuck in it but, I want you to sit with your fear for a moment. Write down what you actually fear in success. Once you do this you can work with it, rather than pushing against it to gain the success you aspire to.

Ask yourself, what do I fear most about success?

Ok. So you are clear on that. Now you can reassure your fear that in working towards success you will not do X, Y or Z?

For example, if you want to run a multi-million pound business you will not lose sight of your freedom within that journey. You will ensure that you have the people and resources around you at each step along the way to maintain a life of freedom. All your decisions in growing the business and bringing people on board will be made with that understanding in mind.

Now you've created a success definition that works. For example, Success is building a life with my freedom at the heart of all I do.

No matter where your life, career or business takes you, no matter how much money you make in the pursuit of that goal if you maintain the freedom that is most important to you, you will feel success. The great thing is if you don't stick to this, your subconscious mind quickly lets you know and you can take action to get back on track!

Another lady said this after her one to one with me. "I've always considered myself to be fairly good at tackling things, getting things done etc. Wow! Yes I was fairly good but Michala taught me how to be REALLY good. Michala doesn't tell you what to do/see/think. Instead, with careful questions she makes you find the way yourself. I went on to do an hour one to one session to create a Success definition. This is so empowering. My simple mantra "Success is thriving" is fully embedded in my daily routines now. If anyone feels they need some clarity no matter how much, I would highly recommend you get in touch with Michala at Wood for the Trees.

THANK YOU MICHALA."

Obviously, there is a lot more to this client's success definition than the 3 words above. It is simply the daily trigger that will keep her on track and focused on whatever she is doing or offered, this is what success means to her now.

Write your success definition somewhere you will see it regularly or say it to yourself on a daily basis. This will keep you mindful of the assurances you made to your fear and support you in making decisions and future planning.

All that remains to say, oh gorgeous one, is I wish you every SUCCESS!! YOUR SUCCESS!!

Conclusion - I can see clearly now the rain has gone.

EEEk it's exciting!! You can do it. You have it in you. You know it. I know it. You've worked your way through the book I hope. (If not, get your ass back to the start and DO THE WORK! Only YOU can make the changes you want for you. Just like I am the only one who can make the changes I need to make for me!)

Now it is time to be a woman of action. Small, daily steps to get you closer to that Big Dream (Jonny Depp, here I come, hope you are ready for me!! WOOOO HOOO!! Ok, so that's more of a fantasy than a dream, but leave me with it!) Are YOU ready to Bounce back?

The great thing is there is reality. This book was a dream. Now it's a reality. You are reading it. You've worked your way through it. (**Seriously**, back to the start and get on with it if you haven't!) I am living my mission of supporting women make positive changes and gain clarity in their lives. That makes me happy. I don't know about you, but as things start to happen for people I work with I can feel the love. One of my Solution Focused Sisters wrote this as we were reviewing how the past few months had changed for her

"Overall it has been a journey, and at the beginning of the year it felt like a journey to hell but I found Michala's challenge and now I have changed path and I am feeling much calmer and happier for it…. Huge thanks to Michala, you have saved me from drowning in the chaos and drama that my life was this year."

In reality she needs to thank herself for doing the work. Being dedicated to finding the space to achieve the clarity and focus she has achieved, and using the Solution Focused approach I teach, to be content in her life.

You can do this too. There will be days when it all feels too much. When the washing pile is over flowing again; when the paper in tray is spilling over; when the inbox storage is full again and you feel like you are drowning in the volume of priorities. You are wearing your busy badge of honour but you aren't sure what you are doing and why? Do you think I don't feel like that sometimes? I'm not a Stepford Wife believe me. I'm not a robot. I wobble. I feel overwhelmed as life events take over; or I reach the next stage of my business; or as my children reach a new stage in their life and I have to work out how to deal with cyberbullying or hormones! (OM giddy aunt! Hormones, what the heck!!)

Life chucks stuff at us (very technical term. LOL). Bereavements, ill health, friends or family falling out, work place politics, lack of sales in your business, the list goes on. It's all there to help us learn and grow. We have to look at it with clear eyes. Eyes that see how hard we are trying. Eyes that see we are good enough, even when we make mistakes or could have handled something better. Eyes that can see daily we are being kind to ourselves so we can give from a place of love.

Burnout happens when we aren't in alignment with what makes us feel successful, and environment can play a big part in this. Use a burnout to see if the environment you are in is helping you thrive or strive. Then get the support and help you need to make the changes you need as well as using the tools this book has provided to keep you high on your mental game, curious to find solutions and resources to look after you.

I believe we are on this planet to achieve success on our own terms in our own way. For you success will be one thing, for me another and that is ok. Life is all about choices and perspective. How you are looking at life will impact on the choices you make. Gain a perspective that is solution focused and the choices you make will be positive with you at the heart of all you do. You have one life. Live it. Love it. Succeed your way. You Can Do IT.

What are you waiting for?

The right conditions, the perfect moment, the right finances, more time?

Your time is now. Do the work. Start seeing the wood…. Bounce back.

"Who created the belief you can't?

Can You?"

Michala Leyland

Thank you

First, to the love of my life for always supporting me and sticking through life's ups and downs with me. My treasures for teaching me things about myself I never knew and for being themselves!

Janine Blythe and Peter Thompson for helping me get to print practically, and emotionally! Nadine Baynes for being a true mate and helping me Awaken. My family & friends for teaching me it's OK to say no and to still be loved.

To my Periscope and Facebook pals, you motivate me every day with your caring, sharing and kick up the backsiding! LOL Finally, to all the clients I've worked with on line and off. Your bravery, resilience and shining lights inspire me to be the best version of me I can be. It's not perfect but it's good enough.

What other choice is there after all?

Bibliography

Chamaine, S. (2015) Positive Intelligence. Greenleaf Book Group Press. Austin TX

Peters, S. (2012) The Chimp Paradox: The Mind Management Programme. Croydon. Vermillion.

Rosenburg, M.B. (2003) Nonviolent Communication: A Language in Life. USA. PuddleDancer Press.

On Line References

Maslach,C. (2016) Retrieved from
https://www.researchgate.net/publication/277816643

 Maslach, C. & Leiter, M.P. Retrieved from
http://www.newchaptercoach.com/wp-content/uploads/2008/11/activist-burnout-article1.pdf

Thorreau, H.D. Retrieved from
 http://quotationsbook.com/quote/5260/

Brown, B. Retrieved from
https://www.youtube.com/watch?v=ecb6ExBaW80

Ziglar, Z. Retrieved from
http://www.goodreads.com/quotes/270489-lack-of-direction- not-lack-of-time-is-the-problem

Nin, A. Retrieved from
https://en.wikiquote.org/wiki/Ana%C3%AFs_Nin

Leyland, M. (2015) Retrieved from
www.woodforthetreescoaching.co.uk

Leyland, M. (2015) Retrieved from
http://www.woodforthetreescoaching.co.uk/blog/5-simple-steps-to-be-your-own-best-friend-forever

Herman, T. & Forleo, M. (2014) Retrieved through
https://www.youtube.com/watch?v=CKLK04IU4Do

Robbins, T. (2013) Retrieved through
https://www.youtube.com/watch?v=4JIzngH9UBQ

Michala Leyland (2015) Retrieved through
http://www.woodforthetreescoaching.co.uk/blog/are-you-the-ceo-in-your-home-top-tips-for-more-productivity-and

http://www.woodforthetreescoaching.co.uk/solution-focused- sisterhood-members-club.html

For more opportunities to connect with the author, follow her on:

Facebook at www.facebook.com/woodforthetreescoaching

Periscope: @wfttcoaching (not wtf!!)

Twitter: @wfttcoaching

Website: www.woodforthetreescoaching.co.uk